Christmas

by Mari C. Schuh

Consulting Editor: Gail Saunders-Smith, Ph.D.

Consultant: Alexa Sandmann, Ed.D.
Professor of Literacy
The University of Toledo
Member, National Council for the Social Studies

Pebble Books

an imprint of Capstone Press
Mankato, Minnesota

Pebble Books are published by Capstone Press,
1710 Roe Crest Drive, North Mankato, Minnesota 56003.
www.capstonepub.com

Library of Congress Cataloging-in-Publication Data
Schuh, Mari C., 1975-
    Christmas / By Mari C. Schuh.
    p. cm.—(Holidays and celebrations)
    Includes bibliographical references and index.
    ISBN-13: 978-0-7368-0979-5 (hardcover)   ISBN-10: 0-7368-0979-1 (hardcover)
    ISBN-13: 978-0-7368-4904-3 (softcover)   ISBN-10: 0-7368-4904-1 (softcover)
    1. Christmas—Juvenile literature. [1. Christmas. 2. Holidays.]
I. Title. II. Series.
GT4985.5 .S38 2002
394.2663—dc21
                         00-012793

Summary: Simple text and photographs describe the history of Christmas and how it is
celebrated.

Note to Parents and Teachers

The Holidays and Celebrations series supports national social studies
standards related to culture. This book describes Christmas and
illustrates how it is celebrated. The photographs support early readers
in understanding the text. The repetition of words and phrases helps
early readers learn new words. This book also introduces early readers to
subject-specific vocabulary words, which are defined in the Words to Know
section. Early readers may need assistance to read some words and to use the
Table of Contents, Words to Know, Read More, Internet Sites, and Index/Word
List sections of the book.

Table of Contents

December

S	M	T	W	T	F	S
1	2	3	4	5	6	7
8	9	10	11	12	13	14
15	16	17	18	19	20	21
22	23	24	(25)	26	27	28
29	30	31				

Christmas is on December 25. Christians celebrate the birth of Jesus on this day.

Jesus was born a little more than 2,000 years ago. Christians believe that Jesus is the son of God.

Many Christians go to church on Christmas. They remember the birth of Jesus. They pray and sing.

Some people write Christmas cards. They wish their friends and families a happy holiday.

Some people eat Christmas treats. They eat Christmas cookies, candy, and gingerbread.

14

Some people decorate
their homes for Christmas.
They hang stockings,
wreaths, and mistletoe.

Some people put Christmas trees in their homes. They hang lights and ornaments on the tree.

Some kids visit Santa Claus. They tell him what they want for Christmas.

20

Friends and family members give Christmas presents to each other. They share the Christmas spirit.

Words to Know

Christian—a person who follows the teachings of Jesus Christ

decorate—to add items to a room or an object to make it look nice

God—creator and ruler of the world and the universe in some religions such as Christianity

Jesus—the founder of a religion called Christianity; Christians believe that Jesus is the son of God.

mistletoe—a plant with white berries that grows on some trees

ornament—a decoration hung on a Christmas tree

Santa Claus—a jolly old man with a white beard and a red suit; Santa Claus is believed to give presents to good children during Christmas.

stocking—a covering for the foot and leg; some people hang Christmas stockings over their fireplaces; they hope that Santa Claus will fill the stockings with gifts.

Read More

Chambers, Catherine. *Christmas.* A World of Holidays. Austin, Texas: Raintree Steck-Vaughn, 1997.

Marx, David F. *Christmas.* Rookie Read-About Holidays. New York: Children's Press, 2000.

Rau, Dana Meachen. *Christmas.* A True Book. New York: Children's Press, 2000.

Internet Sites

FactHound offers a safe, fun way to find Internet sites related to this book. All of the sites on FactHound have been researched by our staff.

Here's all you do:

Visit *www.facthound.com*

FactHound will fetch the best sites for you!

Index/Word List

Word Count: 133
Early-Intervention Level: 13

Credits
Heather Kindseth, cover designer; Kia Bielke, production designer; Kimberly Danger, photo researcher

Capstone Press/Gary Sundermeyer, cover, 1, 4, 10, 12, 18
Photo Network/Myrleen Ferguson Cate, 20
Photri-Microstock, 6
Ron Chapple/FPG International LLC, 16
Susanne Thornburg, 14
Unicorn Stock Photos/Jeff Greenberg, 8